Diary Of A Wimpy Noob:
Fortnite Battle

Check out the _Noob Series_

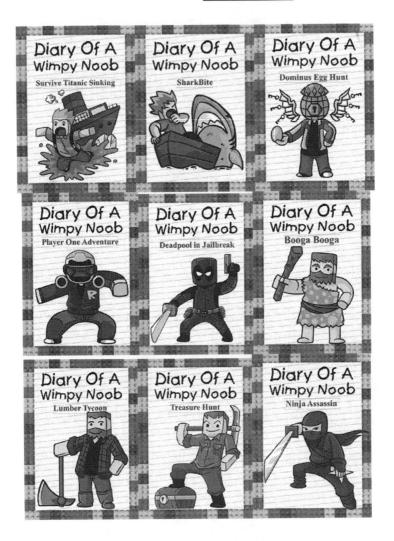

New Releases ➔ _http://amzn.to/2rUEML3_

TABLE OF CONTENTS

PART 1: A STRANGE BUS RIDE

"All aboard!"

The voice of the bus driver rang out over large dirt parking lot. From every direction, Roblox people were hurrying onto the bus. I stood still and stared at the strange contraption as people climbed in. The bus itself was normal enough. It looked a little old and weathered, but still in good condition. It was large too! Larger than a normal bus. My estimation was that it could hold upwards of one hundred people. Judging from the number of people who were going in, I don't think my guess was too far off. What really gave me pause though, was the enormous hot air balloon floating above the bus!

See, this bus wasn't designed to be driven. It was made to fly. And in a few moments, the driver would be taking us to a new Roblox server known simply as Fortnite.

"Mike, why are you standing like a statue? The bus is about to leave?"

My best friend Bruno hurried up to me and shook my shoulders vigorously. He was joined by my other friend, Jenna. It was the two of them that had invited me to come along on this new adventure, and now I was having serious misgivings.

"That bus doesn't exactly look safe guys," I said.

"Mikey," Jenna said, rolling her eyes. "This is a Fortnite server! We're literally trying to shoot each other. It isn't SUPPOSED to be safe! Now let's go!"

Against my better judgment, I followed my friends on board. Several minutes later the bus lurched forward and rose into the air. We soared high into the sky and then began our journey towards the island where the battle would be fought. Everyone on the bus was talking excitedly about the match, but I chose to stare out the window and think.

After a short flight over the ocean, a large green island came slowly into view. Seeing the land approaching made this whole excursion seem suddenly much more real and frightening. I turned to my two friends and spoke nervously.

"So, explain to me again what I'm supposed to do here?"

"First," Jenna said while shoving a large pickax into my hand. "You need to hold onto this. It's your most important tool. Don't lose it!"

Bruno cut in. "Ignore Jenna, that's not your main concern right now. What you need to focus on is finding a safe spot to land and then finding a good gun! It's every man for himself down there! If we see each other we might work together, but it's still a free-for-all!"

"Wait, what did you say about landing? Won't the bus landing us all together?" I asked.

Bruno and Jenna exchanged glances and then burst out laughing.

"Someone is in for a surprise!" Jenna exclaimed.

At that moment a green light flashed inside the bus.

"GO! GO! GO!" a voice shouted.

Before I could react the walls of the bus lifted up and I was violently sucked out! I was free falling through space thousands of feet above the ground! In my terror, I noticed everyone else was doing the same thing.

"Pull the handle on your parachute!" I heard some say as I went plummeting downward.

My parachute! I frantically fumbled around for a handle and managed to find it. Yanking down hard I felt a parachute open overhead, slowing my descent. This was not the beginning I had expected! Several seconds later I crashed down onto the earth. The land around me was silent. It seemed that I was completely alone. Maybe I could find Bruno and Jenna in peace!

PART 2: WELCOME TO THE ISLAND

POW! POW! POW!

A string of shots rang out, and the bullets crashed into the wooden fence a foot away from me, throwing a shower of splinters in my direction. I dove to the ground behind a large rock and covered my head, awaiting another barrage. But no more shots rang out. I glanced to my left and then right. I couldn't see anyone! The landscape as far as I could tell was completely empty. For miles in every direction stretched lush green earth, dotted with large trees and rolling hills. It really was a pristine place to get shot at!

I suddenly realized that I had dropped my pickax! In my haste to get under cover it had slipped from my hands and now lay in the open a few feet away from where I was now hiding. I couldn't leave it! It was the only weapon I possessed! I lay silently for a few more seconds, listening to the birds singing peacefully in the trees. Whoever had shot at me initially seemed to have given up. Perhaps it was now safe to retrieve my tool. I got to my knees and inched my way from cover towards the pickax.

POW! POW! POW! POW!

Bullets whizzed past my head! Several struck the dirt near me and threw large clouds into my face! In my panic, I made a mad dash towards my pickax, somehow managed to grab it, and then half-dove, half-fell into a nearby thicket! As I lay awkwardly, face half crushed into the bushes, I tried to ignore the sharp thorns being driven into my skin. Then I recounted the decisions that had brought me to this place.

Roblox Fortnite: what was I thinking when I decided to come here??

"Mike! What are you doing?" A girl's voice, in a hushed whisper, reached my ears.

I glanced up from where I was laying amidst the brambles and noticed a small red-brick building several yards away. In the corner of one of the windows, I spotted the familiar face of my friend Jenna. She was trying to remain concealed but her light blonde hair was reflecting the afternoon sunshine.

"Jenna," I moaned. "I don't know what I'm doing here. Just put me out of my misery."

"Stop being such a baby, and keep your voice down! Would you like some help?"

"Yes please."

"Okay. I think I know where your being shot from. I'm going to lay down some covering fire and when I do, you need to get your sorry butt into this building. Do you understand?"

"But, what if there's more than one shooter? I could die!"

Jenna sighed. "Mikey, do you want help or not?"

"Yes, Jenna."

"Then do as I say! Ready?"

"No! Don't star-"

"GO!!"

POW! POW! POW!

Before I could prepare, Jenna stood in the window and unleashed a barrage of fire at a spot in the distance. I scrambled to my feet as quickly as I could and dashed towards the brick building. I was nearly to the door when several shots rang out behind me. The bullets thudded into the brick, knocking chunks free dangerously close to my head. Panicked, I leaped forward and flew headlong inside, before skidding across the floor and crashing into a pile of boxes.

"You really know how to make an entrance, don't you?" Jenna said with a playful grin.

PART 3: TIME TO MOVE

I climbed to my feet and brushed the dirt off my clothes. Inside the brick building, no one was firing at me. For the moment at least, I was safe. I looked over at Jenna, who was still manning her post at the window. Unlike me, her pickax was slung over her pack. In her hands, she held an automatic rifle.

"Wow," I exclaimed. "We haven't been on the ground for more than five minutes! Where did you find that?"

"This old thing? These things are laying around everywhere!" Jenna grinned and patted the rifle affectionately.

A voice called out from another room adjacent to ours. "You know she's right. There are guns all over this island! You need to get with the program, Mike!"

Bruno emerged from the side room. He was cradling a sawed-off shotgun in his arm.

"Both of you have guns!? All I've done is get shot at!" I

exclaimed.

"Don't sweat it, buddy," Bruno said. "The learning curve here is pretty steep. Here. You can have my spare."

Bruno reached down with one of his brawny arms and retrieved a small pistol from a holster on his side. He tossed the handgun to me, along with some spare cartridges. Seeing my two friends armed to the teeth while I struggled to hold onto my pickax suddenly made me feel very inadequate.

"I've never even used one of these before," I muttered while fumbling with the pistol.

"So what's our plan? Are we going to cut Mike here a break and work together this time or should I just blast you both right now?" Jenna asked.

"Take it easy, tiger," Bruno chuckled while gripping his shotgun a little tighter. "We'll roll out as a team this time. Otherwise, poor Mike is going to end up dying pretty fast!"

"I appreciate the vote of confidence, guys," I said.

"Anytime!" Bruno answered.

"Well then let's come up with a plan. We landed near the Funky Forest. We could hole up here for a while but eventually, we'll need to upgrade our weapons." Jenna said.

"Agreed. That little pistol of Mike's won't last long against enemies with body armor!" Bruno commented.

"Exactly," said Jenna. "So I think we should head around Lil Lake and over to the Sad Settlement. There are usually some pretty good guns there. If we hurry they won't all be taken yet!"

"I'm on board with that! Mike, are you okay with our plan?" Bruno asked me.

I held my hands up. "Hey guys, I'm along for the ride right now! I'm just thankful no one has shot me yet!"

"You'll be safe with us." Jenna smiled.

Just then we all heard a strange whistling noise outside. I stood to my feet and spoke quizzically.

"I've never heard a bird sing like that bef-"

"RPG!!!!!" Bruno shouted.

Jenna and Bruno both dove to the floor while I stared at them in confusion. At that moment a missile flew through the open window and struck the wall behind us. There was a blinding flash followed by a tremendous explosion that hurled me forward and against the brick wall. Bricks and mortar went flying in every direction as the back half of the building was blown completely open. Above us, the roof creaked and groaned.

"Uhnnnn....." I moaned.

Jenna and Bruno were already back on their feet.

"Come on, Mike! It's time to get going!"

PART 4: GEARING UP

Now that there was a massive, gaping hole in our brick building, there was no shortage of space when it came to getting out. The obvious downside to this fact was that there was also a clear line of sight for anyone who happened to be located on that side of the building. Of course, having been just fired at by an RPG, we weren't too concerned with anything besides escaping. Bruno, Jenna, and I dashed through the breach and went pummeling down a small hill towards a grove of trees. As we ran my mind dimly registered that someone was still shooting at us. I don't know how close the bullets were coming though, thanks to the fact that my ears were still ringing from the RPG explosion moments earlier.

"Take cover in the trees," Jenna shouted to me as we ran. "We aren't far from Lil Lake now!"

After a short sprint, we reached the trees and I found the largest trunk possible to cower behind. Jenna took up watch nearby while Bruno brought up the rear. Bruno was the biggest and strongest of our group, but all the upper body also made him slow. He arrived at our location gasping for breath.

"Anybody hurt?" he asked, panting hard.

"I think we're all good, how about you?" replied Jenna.

"Just winded, that's all. There were a couple close shots but nothing hit me."

"That's a relief," Jenna said. "None of us have any bandages yet! Hopefully, we can find some in the Sad Settlement."

"Speaking of which, should we start heading that way?" I asked. I was feeling extremely exposed, even behind the largest tree.

"Mike is right, we shouldn't linger here. All the good loot will be gone if we don't hurry!" Jenna agreed.

Bruno caught his breath for a few moments and then the

three of us set out. Jenna was the most confident in her land navigation, so she walked at the point. Bruno and I were in a wing formation to her left and right. I was careful not to stray too far from either of my friends since I was certain that if I encountered an enemy I would not know what to do, and most likely just die. Dying was obviously part of this Roblox server, and not to be feared, but I wondered how much it would hurt. The idea of being shot definitely did not sit well with me!

As Jenna had predicted, we found our way quickly to Lil Lake. Upon reaching it, we began to cautiously skirt its edge while moving closer to Sad Settlement. So far, we had not seen anyone. I knew they were out there though because I could hear the echoes of gunfire in the distance. After a few minutes, I saw the shapes of buildings through the trees up ahead. Moving quietly, we approached the small town.

Jenna brought us up along the edge of a small shack on the outskirts, where she planned to scout the town itself. I was crouched in the back, awaiting further instructions, when a piercing scream came from behind me! I turned my head just in time to see a sharp pickax swinging directly for my head! Somehow, I managed to duck at the very last moment, and the sharp point drove deeply into the wall of the shack.

"Bruno! Jenna!" I cried, scrambling backward away from my attacker, while the attacker reached for a weapon slung over his back!

BOOM!

One shot from Bruno's shotgun sent my foe into oblivion.

"You gotta keep your eye out for those melee-kill guys! They'll sneak up on you!" Bruno said.

"On the plus side, he was carrying a gun! It looks like you're getting an upgrade, Mikey! Congratulations!" Jenna laughed.

PART 5: SEARCHING SAD SETTLEMENT

Yet again, my companions had saved my life. I was beginning to feel like little more than extra baggage on this adventure! While Jenna maintained security, Bruno and I rummaged through the belongings of our fallen enemy for anything of value. The first thing Bruno grabbed was a hunting rifle from off the man's back.

"Here," he said. "It's not the greatest weapon out there, but it'll be better in a gunfight than that pistol."

I inspected the rifle. It appeared well used, and a bit rough around the edges, but sturdy. It also had a scope affixed to the barrel which enabled me to gain a clearer picture of enemies at a distance. I slung the rifle over my shoulder and collected all the ammo that the man was carrying. Bruno also found a few bandages, which he stuffed in his cargo pockets, and one more thing of value.

"A hand grenade! This might come in handy!" he exclaimed, examining the small explosive before placing it in his pocket.

"Nice find," Jenna said. "Was there anything else?"

"He had some bandages, but that's it," I answered.

"Alright, well we should get moving then. Time is passing fast and I don't want to stay out here too long."

With the search over the three of us picked up and began to sweep through Sad Settlement. We stayed close together, with Jenna again leading at the front, and Bruno vigilantly watching our rear. We moved with extreme caution and stayed as quiet as possible, but ultimately it proved unnecessary. The village was a ghost town. But it was obvious that there had been a serious conflict here recently. There were bullet holes, large and small, across many of the buildings, as well as singed earth from numerous explosions. I was grateful that we had missed the majority of the action. Unfortunately, it meant that the settlement had already been picked clean of valuable supplies.

"Well, this was a bust," Jenna said after we had made our

way through the deserted town.

"Pretty much," agreed Bruno. "But at least we're still alive. And Mike has a better weapon! So it isn't all bad!"

"Fair enough. Mike, do feel comfortable with that rifle?"

I pulled it off my shoulder and looked it over again.

"I think it'll work better for me than the pistol would have. Also, I like this scope! I think it'll help me a lot with my accuracy!"

"It will," agreed Bruno. "As long as you don't let the bad guys sneak up on you like the last one!"

THUMP! THUMP! THUMP!

Bruno's teasing was interrupted by the sound of heavy bullets striking the wall of the wood structure we were standing next to. The bullets were coming from the opposite side of the building, but the force was so powerful that they were being driven straight through! All three of us ducked for cover.

"Someone must have seen our sweep through the settlement! And from the sounds of it, they're well armed!" Jenna exclaimed.

THUMP! THUMP! CRACK!

More shots rang out, and one bullet tore straight through the wall! Bruno inched to the corner of the building and peeked around.

POW! POW! POW!

A flurry of shots came whizzing in our direction and Bruno dove back.

"Bad news guys! There's a full squad of them, and they're trying to flank us!"

"Okay, so if we don't move we'll be flanked, and fighting is out of the question. I guess that leaves one option." Jenna said.

She grabbed the pickax from off her shoulder, as did Bruno.

"Okay boys," Jenna cried. "Time to do some building!"

PART 6: ESCAPE TO THE WOODS

I watched in stunned fascination as Jenna and Bruno set to work with their pickaxes. First, they set about deconstructing wall immediately adjacent to us. After just a few powerful blows the wall had collapsed into nothing more than a pile of lumber. Then, they began transforming the lumber into a more suitable purpose. They were crafting portable wooden walls! Feeling that the walls would need support, Bruno dashed into the now partially deconstructed building and retrieved some metal bars, which he then used to reinforce the wood panels and make them more durable. When it was all said and done, I was looking at three large, yet mobile sheets. And the most shocking fact was that the process only lasted a minute or so!

POW! POW!

Several shots whizzed close by, and one of them struck the top of one of the panels.

"I think that's a sign that we've lingered here too long!" I shouted nervously.

"I think you're right, Mike," Jenna said. "Everyone grab a panel and let's start moving out of here!"

Bruno and Jenna each hefted one of the panels and proceeded to use it as a shield while they hurried out of Sad Settlement. Not wanting to be left behind, I grabbed the last one and raced to catch up! The wood sheets were large and rather obtuse, but it wasn't too difficult to keep it properly positioned in order to obstruct the shot of our enemies. I suppose we are all capable of impressive things when our lives are in danger!

The three of us were clear of Sad Settlement in just a matter of moments and beating a hasty retreat back towards Lil Lake and the surrounding woods. But our pursuers were not letting us get off easily! They were closing in fast and firing at us frequently as we moved away. While the wooden walls were good for protection, they also made it impossible for us to see what the other people were doing!

CRACK! CRACK! POW!

To my surprise, shots came flying by me from behind! Realizing the situation, I quickly alerted the others.

"They're still trying to flank around us!" I shouted out.

"Mike! Get in close to Bruno and turn your shield towards the back!" Jenna called back.

It was a brilliant strategy. Bruno and I formed an L shape, with my shield covering our rear and Bruno's obstructing the side. It didn't come a moment too soon either. I had only just changed the shield to my back when several shots rang out. Two of them hit my wooden shield, and the force nearly knocked me to my feet!

"Keep moving buddy! We're almost out of this!" Bruno encouraged.

Bruno spoke true. As we hurried deeper into the woods the frequency of shots became less and less, until it died off completely. By the time we had reached Lil Lake, I felt reasonably safe again.

"I think we're safe," Jenna announced, dropping her shield to the ground. "It looks like we lost them!"

"Thank goodness," I exclaimed, tossing mine to the ground as well. "My arms felt like they were on fire!"

"Same here! But we can't linger here too long. The odds are that they're going to be coming this way, and I don't want to fight them in the forest!" Bruno said.

CRACK!!

Just then a single shot rang out through the trees. We were all too stunned to move! But what I saw next shocked me even more. Jenna suddenly went pale. She clutched at her chest, and then slowly slumped to the ground.

Jenna had been shot!

PART 7: IMMEDIATE EVACUATION

"Jenna!" I screamed as my friend collapsed to her knees.

Her hand had gone to a spot high on her chest, and I could see the fabric of her shirt turning a dark red beneath her fingers.

"Quick," Bruno cried. "Get her behind some cover!"

The two of us dragged her behind a thick tree trunk. As we did, another loud shot could be heard from further back in the forest. The bullet was well-aimed, and lodged itself deeply in the tree we were now cowering behind!

"It looks like we didn't outrun them after!" I said bitterly.

"Perhaps, or perhaps not," Bruno replied, while anxiously scanning the perimeter around us.

"What do you mean?"

"Those shots are coming from a very high-powered rifle, that's all. I didn't hear those kinds of bullets being fired while we were leaving Sad Settlement. It could be someone else."

"So, just another random guy trying to kill us?"

"Exactly," Bruno said, eyeing me closely. "That is the point of this Roblox server, you know. It's a last-man-standing Battle Royale. I think that we might be getting attacked by a sniper."

"Alright, I understand. So what's our course of action?"

"Well, we can't stay here, that's for sure. That sniper is probably watching us through his scope right now!"

"What about our shields?" I asked.

"No good. I'm going to have to carry Jenna and we don't know exactly where the sniper is, so it'll be pointless for you to try and run with the shields again. He could be anywhere."

Bruno reached down and pulled the automatic rifle from off of Jenna's shoulder then handed it to me.

"Here's what we'll do: I'm going to run like a madman with Jenna on my shoulder. We'll head for the Freaky Fields, just west of here. You're going to provide covering fire for us, okay?"

"But I don't know where the sniper is!" I protested.

"Mike! I don't need you to hit the guy, I just need you to keep his head down while we move. It's not a great plan but Jenna is bleeding out and I can't patch her up here! You have to do this!"

I looked down at Jenna. The bloodstain on her shirt was growing wider. She was still alive, but her breathing was heavy and labored. I knew that she didn't have much time.

"Alright," I sighed. "Let's do it."

"Okay. Get to work, Mike."

At Bruno's command, I swung out and around the tree trunk and unleashed a hail of bullets out into the forest in the direction I thought the sniper had fired from.

POW! POW! POW! POW! POW!

The force of the rifle was so violent that it made it difficult for me to stand straight. The barrel of the gun shook wildly, sending bullets in every direction. I supposed this was a good thing since I had no idea where my target was! Bruno reached down scooped up Jenna in his massive arms. He tossed her onto his shoulders with ease and began sprinting away. I followed along as best I could while still firing bullets back the way we came. The plan seemed to be working!

Feeling a growing sense of confidence, I shouted out at the sniper. "Not today buddy! Not today!"

PART 8: SAVING JENNA

To my great surprise, Bruno's scheme worked! My erratic gunfire seemed to do the trick because we didn't receive any more fire from the sniper as we made our way out of the forest. We were both in a desperate hurry to get away from Lil Lake and Funky forest, but our progress was slow. Bruno was a big guy, and moving fast wasn't one of his strengths, to begin with. But when he was carrying another person on his back he became even slower. Still, we did our best and after some time we were finally clear of the woods and once more in a place of relative safety.

Freaky Fields was a wide expanse that featured extensive sight lines with very few obstructions. There were a few scraggly trees and bushes, as well as some small shacks dotting the landscape, but for the most part, it was wide open. Having just been shot at by a sniper, I felt extremely exposed as we made our way across the fields, but thankfully no one took a crack at Bruno or myself. We located a run-down hut not far from the forest and Bruno headed directly for it. Once we got there, my companion had me go inside first to check for threats. Once this task was completed, Bruno brought Jenna inside and began treatment while I took up a lookout position at the door.

"Alright, Jenna," Bruno said. "Let's get you patched up!"

He retrieved the bandages that we had scavenged from Sad Settlement and began to tightly wind them over Jenna's wounded chest. She winced slightly, but almost immediately began to show signs of healing!

"Wow," I commented. "What do they put in those bandages?"

"That's the beauty of Roblox. You can make just about anything happen on a server!" Bruno replied, grinning.

It wasn't long until Jenna was almost back to full health. While she recovered, I continued to scan the horizon for any threats. I was starting to feel pretty good about myself and our situation. For the first time since I landed on this island, I was actually contributing to our success! It made me feel a lot more confident about the whole ordeal. Maybe

I wouldn't die here after all!

"Hey, Mike. Thanks for covering for me back there!" Jenna said, walking up to me.

She looked great now and was smiling broadly at me.

"Not a problem," I answered, that's what friends are for!"

"Exactly. I think I'm good to carry my rifle now though."

"Oh! Of course!" I handed her the rifle and retrieved my own from off of my back.

"Thanks! Have you seen anything?"

"Not yet. The place has been pretty empty!"

"What that's over there?" Bruno asked.

We all turned to look where he was pointing. Far across the fields, we spotted five people. They looked heavily armed and were running quickly. One of them looked like he was carrying a sniper rifle.

"That's them," Jenna growled. "Those are the people who attacked us. And it looks like the sniper is working with them after all!"

"They aren't headed this way," I noted. "I wonder where they're going."

"They're going to Topsy Towers. That's the center of the map. But we're going to meet them there. It's time for a little payback!"

PART 9: STORMS ON THE HORIZON

The sight of our attackers moving across the open fields seemed to have lit a fire under Jenna. She seemed totally consumed with the idea of hunting them down and exacting revenge. This was not a bad thing though. After all, the whole point of this Roblox server was to kill your opponents! Personally, I was grateful to have such good companions with me on this adventure. I could only imagine how difficult this would be, or how quickly I would have died had it not been for Jenna and Bruno!

Jenna had a plan set firmly in her mind and we wasted little time in setting out for Topsy Towers. Twisty Towers was the largest group of structures on the island, and was the most centrally located. From Freaky Fields I could easily see the large buildings that loomed out over the landscape. Even from a distance, I could tell that it would be a dangerous place to fight due to the closeness of the buildings and the excellent sightlines the tall towers provided. It seemed then to me that it would be extremely important that we reached the towers before anyone else did. If we were caught in these open fields, it would be perilous attempting to cross.

Freaky Fields was not far from Topsy Towers and we were able to reach it without incident. However, as we approached it became apparent that we would not be the first to reach the location. From within the buildings I could already hear the loud echoes of gunshots.

"It sounds like things are going to get interesting!" Jenna called back over her shoulder.

We picked up our pace. So far, none of the shots had been fired at us, but none of us wanted to be out in the open longer than necessary. We sprinted the last few yards and crept up alongside one of the tall buildings on the outskirts.

"Well," Bruno said, panting heavily. "It would seem that we'll have some company!"

"It may have been a good thing for us. Whoever was here already has been slowing down the advance of those other people. If we play our cards right, we can come in from behind and clear the towers and then use the height advantage to eliminate everyone else!" Jenna exclaimed.

"Whatever we do, let's do it quickly. The weather is starting to look pretty ominous." I said.

Bruno and Jenna looked up, only now noticing what I had seen while crossing Freaky Fields. The sky had shifted from a radiant blue into a deep purple shade. Angry clouds were billowing in from all directions, creating what looked like a wall around the landscape and growing ever smaller by the minute.

"Huh. That's peculiar," said Bruno, looking at the spectacle. "I've never seen anything like that before!"

"You mean this isn't a common occurrence on this server?" I asked, growing more anxious.

"No, it isn't. But the people who operate this Roblox server have been known to do some strange things." Bruno replied.

"Okay, the weather is fascinating, but let's focus on the task at hand," Jenna interjected. "We have some buildings full of dad guys that we need to take care of. I don't know about you two, but I want to win this match! Now let's get to work!"

PART 10: TAKING TOPSY TOWERS

As the dark storm clouds rolled in on us, Bruno, Jenna and myself began our assault on Topsy Towers. Jenna's assessment of the situation had been spot-on. There were indeed several people holed up on the upper levels of some of the buildings. They had spotted the other band of players heading their direction and had focused all of their time and attention on them. Their gunfire had effectively pinned the group down behind a grassy knoll just outside of Topsy Towers, and that was where they were when we began our attack from the backside. The one thing we had not counted on, however was the fact that not everyone within Topsy Towers was working on the same side! What we walked into was essentially a gunfight between three or four different factions!

"Say hello to my little friend!" Bruno shouted, as he strolled into one of the rooms.

BOOM!!

One blast from his shotgun sent a very surprised opponent flying back and up against a wall. The sound of the shotgun caught the attention of another man in a building across the street. He stopped shooting the guys behind the grassy knoll and unleashed a string of bullets at us!

RAT-TAT-TAT!!

The bullets flew into the room and then ricocheted off the walls several times while the three of us dove for cover!

POW!

Another man came running into our room with his weapon drawn and without aiming; I fired a single shot from my rifle that struck him square in the gut!

"I got one! I got my first kill!" I shouted excitedly.

"Nice one," shouted Bruno, smiling broadly. "Everybody get down! I'm going to use my hand grenade on that dude in the other building!"

"Wait," cried Jenna. "We might need it later! We'll take that guy out together."

Bruno gave Jenna a rather surprised look but he complied with her command. Under Jenna's direction, we began an effort to clear out the last remaining man from Topsy Towers. She instructed me to join her in laying down a heavy base of fire from our building in order to distract our opponent while Bruno crept into the opposing structure. We maintained our shooting until we heard the telltale boom of Bruno's shotgun that indicated that the job was done. A few seconds later, we saw his smiling face from the opposite building and we rushed across to join him.

"Well, that job is done!" he exclaimed with a smile.

"We aren't out of the woods yet! Look!" I cried, pointing out to the grassy knoll where the other group of men had been hunkered down. While we had been busy killing off the people in Topsy Towers, we had also inadvertently been killing the people who had been suppressing our enemies! Now that they were free to move again without being attacked, they were rushing to reach Topsy Towers too!

"Quickly," cried Jenna, "We need to kill them before they reach the buildings!"

All of us rushed to windows that lined the walls and took aim on the men below. I had one in my sights and was about to pull the trigger when I heard a peculiar whistling noise, unlike any I had heard before. Bruno and Jenna heard it too, and paused. It was coming from overhead! We all looked skyward and, to our dismay, saw a massive meteor burning down from the sky! Moments later, it crashed to earth not far from Topsy Towers! The sky was now completely covered in dark clouds, and more meteors were following the first.

"Uh, guys. I think we have bigger problems than those people down below." Jenna said slowly.

PART 11: FALLING SKIES

It now appeared as if the entire sky was falling in on us. While the three of us had been busy taking out the people in Topsy Towers the storm clouds had completely enveloped the island in a thick canopy. Instead of pouring rain down upon the land, this storm was raining fire and brimstone in the form of flaming meteors! The first one had killed the group of attackers who were approaching our position, but more meteors were falling closely behind! It seemed as if it would only be a matter of time before one hit us.

"So you're telling me that you've never seen this before? How many times have you been on this Roblox server?" I asked.

"Probably half a dozen times," Bruno said. "But this is all new to me!"

BOOM!!!!!!

A flaming meteor struck the building we had been in just a few minutes earlier! The size and force of the space rock drove it through the roof, all the way to the ground. Needless to say, there was very little left of the building afterwards, other than piles of rubble and debris.

BOOM!! BOOM!!

More giant space rocks were racing to earth now, and the power of the impact was violently shaking the ground and forcing me to grab onto the wall for stability or fall over!

"We can't stay here!" exclaimed a frightened Bruno.

"I'm with him! We need to go somewhere else quickly!" I shouted.

Together, the three of us bounded out of our building and began a mad dash away from Topsy Towers.

BOOM!!

Glancing over my shoulder, I saw that a falling meteor had struck the tower we had just left! I breathed a sigh of relief that we had gotten out in time and then, while my head was still turned, ran smack into the back of Bruno, who had suddenly stopped short.

"Why are we stop-" I cut myself short when I saw what had brought both Jenna and Bruno to a halt. From out of the storm clouds in every direction were the remaining players of this Roblox Fortnite match! They were fleeing from the storm towards the central part of the island where things were not quite as bad yet, despite the torrent of meteors, which were now falling!

POW! POW! POW!

Even as the world was falling down upon us all, many of the people were still stopping to fight with one another! They were shooting one another in the back as they ran for safety and even taking sporadic shots at us! We ducked behind some wooden debris to discuss our situation.

"Okay. So running for our lives is now out of the question. So what now?" asked Jenna.

"There's always the option where we simply sit here and await death." Bruno said sarcastically.

"I don't suppose building shields will help us this time!" I joked, kick at the wood we were hunkered behind.

Bruno and Jenna looked at one another.

"It just might work!" Jenna cried, grabbing her pickax.

"Wait, are you serious?" I asked, astonished.

"Maybe," Bruno cried, frantically following Jenna's lead. "It's worth a shot at the least."

"But those towers didn't stand a chance against the meteors!"

"We don't have to build something that can withstand the full force of the rocks," Jenna said, already busy building. "We just need something that can deflect the blow and hopefully protect us in the process! Now, if you're done asking questions maybe you can help us build, Mike!"

PART 12: UNEXPECTED ENDINGS

Spurred on by my friend's sense of urgency, I jumped in to assist in this impromptu building project. I had never built on any Roblox server that I had ever been on, but I was still surprised at how quickly I picked up the skill! I will be the first to admit that the things I was building were not of high quality, but at this point we were simply desperate to get protection of some sort erected, so overall craftsmanship was not vitally important.

The process for building our defensive structure was remarkably simple. Jenna served as our resource gatherer. She raced back and forth from the destroyed buildings in our vicinity, collecting materials and returning them to our location so that we could erect our defense more quickly. All the while, the intensity of the storm increased, as did the amount of gunfire from the remaining players in the game.

The three of us built frantically, dodging bullets and trying to maintain our balance as the earth around us trembled from the force of impacting meteors. Somehow, we managed to build our shelter higher and higher, in spite of the attacks from the people around us. After we had erected a structure fairly high into the sky Jenna called out.

"Okay! That is all we have time for! Now, get to the bottom floor and hope for the best!"

We followed Jenna's commands, scrambled to the bottom, and hunkered together, waiting for the worst of the storm to pass. All around us the earth shook violently, and overhead I could hear portions of our tower being torn away by falling meteors! Finally, after what seemed like an eternity, the sounds died away.

When I finally dared open my eyes, I found that our tower had been completely destroyed. All around us was nothing but carnage and destruction. It had been a violent storm, and it looked as if everyone but us had died. But we were still alive!!

"Is that it? Is the game over?" I asked, quizzically.

"It should be," Bruno said slowly. "I've never actually survived until the end!"

"But shouldn't there be some sort of sign or signal letting us know that we've won?"

"There will be," Jenna said, walking from behind Bruno and me to a pile of wreckage a few feet away. "Unfortunately, the game isn't over yet. This is a battle royale, meaning the game only ends when one person is left alive."

Bruno and I stared blankly at Jenna while she gave us a sly grin.

"Oh you can't be serious," moaned Bruno. "After all we've been through you want us to try and kill each other?"

Jenna laughed. "Of course not! It's already too late for you two!"

"Huh?" I said dumbly.

"Bruno, look in your pocket."

Bruno's hand shot down to his pocket and he pulled out the hand grenade he had been saving this whole time. To our surprise, the detonating pin had been removed, and it was now hanging off Jenna's finger!

"Jenna. You litt-"

BOOOM!!!!

Bruno never finished his sentence. A split second later both of us were sitting back in the lobby, along with all the other people who had been killed, watching Jenna celebrate her victory.

"Well, it looks like she played us good!" Bruno chuckled.

"I agree, but she won't get so lucky next time! I'm ready for a rematch!"

Thank you for reading *Diary Of A Wimpy Noob:*

Fortnite Battle

I hope you enjoyed it! If you did, help other

people find this by <u>writing a review</u>.

➔ <u>http://amzn.to/2s7tgf5</u>

New releases

Diary Of A Wimpy Pirate 1 ➔ <u>https://amzn.to/2HHM0pr</u>

Diary Of A Wimpy Pirate 2 ➔ <u>https://amzn.to/2jRVILi</u>

Other Authors that I like:

Check out the <u>Diary of a Minecraft Warrior Series</u>

Get the entire series here:
<u>http://amzn.to/2ri8JD3</u>

Are you a Zelda Fan? Then Check out some of these

Have you Ever wonder what it would be like to be a Link? for Real? *Tap*

Here to download: http://amzn.to/2nd4Kp4

Paperback Edition here: http://amzn.to/2nUwMTI

Tap Here to download: http://amzn.to/2nUMyhl

Paperback here: http://amzn.to/2mZqH9d

Are you a fan of Minecraft? Check this out

Diary of a minecraft Evoker series ➜ *http://amzn.to/2zUqyKe*

Are you a Fan of Undertale? Then Check out some of these

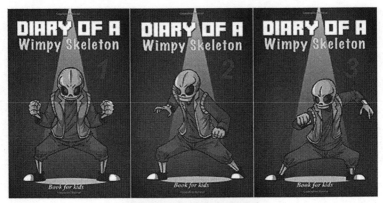

Follow Sans the skeleton and his monster friends who try to situate themselves back into the human society with the help of Frisk and some new human friends.

Get ready for fast-paced exciting adventures complete with funny Jokes and Puns.

Diary of a Wimpy Skeleton series ➔

https://amzn.to/2s1fk3E

Made in the USA
Lexington, KY
28 July 2018